First World War
and Army of Occupation
War Diary
France, Belgium and Germany

2 DIVISION
5 Infantry Brigade
Queen's (Royal West Surrey Regiment)
1st Battalion
1 January 1915 - 31 December 1915

WO95/1350/3

The Naval & Military Press Ltd
www.nmarchive.com
Published in association with The National Archives

Published by

The Naval & Military Press Ltd

Unit 10 Ridgewood Industrial Park,

Uckfield, East Sussex,

TN22 5QE England

Tel: +44 (0) 1825 749494

www.naval-military-press.com

www.nmarchive.com

This diary has been reprinted in facsimile from the original. Any imperfections are inevitably reproduced and the quality may fall short of modern type and cartographic standards.

© Crown Copyright
Images reproduced by permission of The National Archives, London, England, 2015.

Contents

Document type	Place/Title	Date From	Date To
Heading	2nd Division 5th Infy Bde 1st Battalion Royal West Surreys Jan-Dec 1915 From 1 Div 3 Bde to 100 Bde 33 Division Jan 1916		
Heading	War Diary 1st Battalion Royal West Surreys January 1915		
War Diary	Hinges	01/01/1915	03/01/1915
War Diary	Bethune	03/01/1915	11/01/1915
War Diary	Givenchy	12/01/1915	14/01/1915
War Diary	Bethune	15/01/1915	25/01/1915
War Diary	Hinges	26/01/1915	31/01/1915
Heading	War Diary 1st Battalion Royal Surreys February 1915		
War Diary	Hinges	01/02/1915	03/02/1915
War Diary	Choques	04/02/1915	28/02/1915
Heading	War Diary 1st Battalion Royal West Surreys March 1915		
War Diary	Chocques	01/03/1915	09/03/1915
War Diary	Pont Levis	10/03/1915	12/03/1915
War Diary	Bethune	13/03/1915	31/03/1915
Operation(al) Order(s)	1st Corps Operation Order No.70	09/03/1915	09/03/1915
Miscellaneous	A Form Messages And Signals		
Miscellaneous	O.C. 1st Queen Regt.	11/03/1915	11/03/1915
Miscellaneous	A Form Messages And Signals		
Heading	War Diary 1st Battn. The Queen's (Royal West Surrey Regiment). April 1915		
War Diary	Bethune	01/04/1915	09/04/1915
War Diary	Hamel	10/04/1915	30/04/1915
Heading	War Diary 1st Battn. The Queen's (Royal West Surrey Regiment). May 1915		
War Diary	Le Hamel	01/05/1915	08/05/1915
War Diary	N.E. Bethune	09/05/1915	10/05/1915
War Diary	Vendin Lez Bethune	11/05/1915	15/05/1915
War Diary	N.E Bethune	16/05/1915	31/05/1915
Miscellaneous	Appendices XXII & XXIII		
Operation(al) Order(s)	1st Corps Operation Order No.79	07/05/1915	07/05/1915
Operation(al) Order(s)	1st Corps Operation Order No. 83	14/05/1915	14/05/1915
Heading	War Diary 1st Battn.The Queen's (Royal West Surrey Regiment) June 1915		
War Diary	Marles Les Mines	01/06/1915	25/06/1915
War Diary	Beuvry	26/06/1915	30/06/1915
Heading	War Diary 1st Battn. The Queen's (Royal West Surrey Regiment). July 1915		
War Diary	Beuvry	01/07/1915	20/07/1915
War Diary	Bethune	21/07/1915	24/07/1915
War Diary	Trenches (Cuinchy)	25/07/1915	29/07/1915
War Diary	Annequin	30/07/1915	31/07/1915
Heading	War Diary 1st Battn. The Queen's (Royal West Surrey Regiment) August 1915		
War Diary	Annequin	01/08/1915	02/08/1915
War Diary	Cuinchy (Trenches)	03/08/1915	07/08/1915
War Diary	Vendin Les Bethune	08/08/1915	15/08/1915

War Diary	Le Quesnoy	15/08/1915	19/08/1915
War Diary	Sec B2 Givenchy (in trenches)	20/08/1915	24/08/1915
War Diary	Le Quesnoy	24/08/1915	28/08/1915
War Diary	N.E. Bethune	29/08/1915	31/08/1915
Heading	War Diary 1st Battn. The Queen's (Royal West Surrey Regiment). September 1915		
War Diary	N.E. Bethune	01/09/1915	03/09/1915
War Diary	Section B3 Givenchy	04/09/1915	06/09/1915
War Diary	Le Quesnoy	07/09/1915	08/09/1915
War Diary	Section B.3.	09/09/1915	10/09/1915
War Diary	Le Quesnoy	11/09/1915	12/09/1915
War Diary	N.E. Bethune	13/09/1915	16/09/1915
War Diary	Section B2	17/09/1915	22/09/1915
War Diary	Le Quesnoy	23/09/1915	23/09/1915
War Diary	Section B2	24/09/1915	26/09/1915
War Diary	Le Preol	27/09/1915	28/09/1915
War Diary	Beuvry	29/09/1915	30/09/1915
Heading	War Diary 1st Battn. The Queen's (Royal West Surrey Regiment). October 1915		
War Diary		01/10/1915	05/10/1915
War Diary	Avelette	06/10/1915	10/10/1915
War Diary	In The Trenches	11/10/1915	14/10/1915
War Diary	Annequin	15/10/1915	21/10/1915
War Diary	Vendin	22/10/1915	28/10/1915
War Diary	Sector Z1 Cambrin	29/10/1915	31/10/1915
Heading	War Diary 1st Battn. The Queen's (Royal West Surrey Regiment). November 1915		
War Diary	Section Z1 Cambrin	01/11/1915	02/11/1915
War Diary	Annezin	03/11/1915	07/11/1915
War Diary	Annequin	08/11/1915	10/11/1915
War Diary	In The Trenches	10/11/1915	12/11/1915
War Diary	Beuvry	13/11/1915	14/11/1915
War Diary	Vendin	15/11/1915	22/11/1915
War Diary	Harley St. (N. Cambrin)	23/11/1915	25/11/1915
War Diary	Section A 1	26/11/1915	30/11/1915
Heading	War Diary 1st Battn. The Queen's (Royal West Surrey Regiment). December 1915		
War Diary	Bethune	01/12/1915	01/12/1915
War Diary	B1 Section	02/12/1915	06/12/1915
War Diary	Bethune	07/12/1915	07/12/1915
War Diary	Section A 1	08/12/1915	11/12/1915
War Diary	Beuvry	12/12/1915	12/12/1915
War Diary	Bethune	13/12/1915	15/12/1915
War Diary	St Hilaire	16/12/1915	28/12/1915
War Diary	Bethune	29/12/1915	31/12/1915

2ND DIVISION
5TH INFY BDE

WO95
1350

1ST BATTALION
ROYAL WEST SURREYS
JAN – DEC 1915

FROM 1 DIV 3 BDE

TO 100 BDE 33 DIVISION JAN 1916

I Corps Troops.

WAR DIARY

1st Battalion ROYAL WEST SURREYS

January

1915

WAR DIARY or INTELLIGENCE SUMMARY.

Army Form C. 2118.

(Erase heading not required.)

Hour, Date, Place	Summary of Events and Information	Remarks and references to Appendices
HINGES.		
1st January 1915.	Ordinary Routine.	
2nd "	" "	
3rd BETHUNE.	Cleaned up billets. Paraded off at 10 a.m. and went into billets at BETHUNE.	(ARRAS MAP)
4th "	Ordinary Routine.	
5th "	" "	
6th "	" "	
7th "	— Lieut H.E.A. HODGSON joined the Battn for duty.	Battn Organized as follows:—
	Present Strength of Battn 27 Officers — including 1 Medical Officer and [the Rev. J. BLACKBOURNE, Chaplain (to 1st A. Corps (attached)] — and 454 3 C.O's and men. (including attached.)	H.Q. 4 O's, 24pts, 1 pr. H.P. = 53 A Coy 10 " 7 " 7 " 1D,15P = 178 B " 10 " 6 " 5 " — 171 = 192 3. gun D.S. 1 " 1 " — 15 " = 17 " " " " 11 = 14
	Of the above :— 1 Officer, 7 3 C.O's & 62 P.ts are at Army H.Q.	270 6 234t 134t 1bn 390P = 454
	4 " 12 " 55 " are attached at BETHUNE Attached 2 " 1 "	
	22 " 337 " at Regtl 2nd H.Qrs.	
	Daily grand duties employ:—	
	— 8 3 C.O's and 36 P.ts	
	Detailed at night 4 " 10 "	
	Employed at 15t C.H.Q.1 " 14 "	
	13 " 60 "	

Forms/C. 2118/11.

WAR DIARY
or
INTELLIGENCE SUMMARY.
(Erase heading not required.)

Army Form C. 2118.

Instructions regarding War Diaries and Intelligence Summaries are contained in F. S. Regs., Part II. and the Staff Manual respectively. Title pages will be prepared in manuscript.

Hour, Date, Place	Summary of Events and Information	Remarks and references to Appendices
BETHUNE.		1/2
8th January	Ordinary Routine	
9th "	" "	
10th "	" "	
11th "	Divine Service in local Theatre at 11.0 a.m.	
	Left Billets at 4 p.m. and marched via PONT FIXE	Strength of Battn marching
	to GIVENCHY where the Battn relieved 1st Coldstream Gds	out :- 19 Officers (including 2 M.O)
	and 1st London Section in trenches. Sniping intermittently	and 268 men available for
	all night.	duty in the trenches.
GIVENCHY		
12th "	Shelling during morning, but out in our area.	
	Fairly quiet all day. Casualties 1 wounded.	
13th "	Fairly quiet all day with the exception of sniping	In period 11th to 14th the Battn
	Casualties 1 Slightly wounded	was placed at disposal of 1st(?) Bde
14th "	Sniping all day. 1st Gds returned by 7.30 p.m. at 7 p.m.	On the 14th the Battn returned
	The WELCH REGT took over from the Battn. Heavy firing	to Corps troops.
	during relief but no casualties.	
BETHUNE		
15th "	Ordinary Routine. The following Officers joined the Battn in relation	gas cart
	2nd Lt C W ELTHAM, 2nd Lt TWEEDIE-SMITH, 2nd Lt L HEYES, 2nd Lt J BOURSELL	

Army Form C. 2118.

WAR DIARY
or
INTELLIGENCE SUMMARY.
(Erase heading not required.)

Instructions regarding War Diaries and Intelligence Summaries are contained in F.S. Regs., Part II. and the Staff Manual respectively. Title pages will be prepared in manuscript.

Hour, Date, Place	Summary of Events and Information	Remarks and references to Appendices
BETHUNE.		
16th January	Ordinary Routine	
17" "	Divine service in the Theatre at 11 a.m.	
18" "	Ordinary Routine	The Rev. J. BLACKBURN and Lieut. WALSH R.A.M.C. proceeded to England on 7 days leave.
19" "	" "	
20" "	" "	
21" "	" "	
22" "	" "	2nd Lt. LE BAS left the Battn. to join the R.F. Corps.
23" "	" "	
24" "	2nd Lt LE BAS proceeded to ST OMER to join the R.F. Corps.	
25" "	Divine Service at 10.30 a.m. in the Theatre. The Town was shelled from 7.15 a.m. to 9.30 a.m. Many shells failed to explode. No casualties. The Batt'n. paraded at 2.30 p.m and marched to HINGES where we went into our new billets. Reinforcement of 8 Officers 5 Cpls. 14 L/Cpls & 77 P.T.Os. joined this evening.	
HINGES.		
26" "	Ordinary Routine. Received orders at 6 p.m to be ready to move at one hours notice during the night.	Lt. THOMPSON 6/R.Dub. Fus: arrived sickness. Capt.

Army Form C. 2118.

WAR DIARY
or
INTELLIGENCE SUMMARY.
(Erase heading not required.)

Instructions regarding War Diaries and Intelligence Summaries are contained in F. S. Regs., Part II. and the Staff Manual respectively. Title pages will be prepared in manuscript.

Hour, Date, Place	Summary of Events and Information	Remarks and references to Appendices
HINGES		
27th January.	Ordinary Routine by day. Ready to move at an hours notice by night	
28 " "	" " " " " " " "	
29 " "	" " " " " " " "	One Officer and 23 O.R.'s men proceeded to CHOQUES with 1st Line H.T. Ani.
30 " "	Ordinary Routine	
31 " "	— " —	

JMS Capt.
1/2

I Corps Troops.

WAR DIARY

1st Battalion ROYAL WEST SURREYS

February

1915

Army Form C. 2118.

WAR DIARY
or
INTELLIGENCE SUMMARY.
(Erase heading not required.)

Instructions regarding War Diaries and Intelligence Summaries are contained in F. S. Regs., Part II. and the Staff Manual respectively. Title pages will be prepared in manuscript.

Hour, Date, Place	Summary of Events and Information	Remarks and references to Appendices
HINGES.		
1st February 1915.	Ordinary Routine in morning. Received orders from 1st Div. to place 2 Companies at disposal of 1st Divn. today. These 2 Cos. proceeded to BETHUNE at 1.30 p.m. to report to 1st Divn. Regt. H.Q. and Machine Gun Section remained at HINGES.	
2nd February.	The above 2 Cos. employed on placing a house close to PONT FIXE × in a state of defence and constructing a bridgehead line of defence.	× S of FINCHY.
3rd "	Reg. 1st H. Cos. and M. gun Det. moved into C.HOQUES during the afternoon. B Co. returned to billets here at 6.30 p.m.	Three Companies reinforced the ? by a third continued working on new line defences until the end of February.
C.HOQUES.		
4th February.	Cleaned up billets all day. A Co. rejoined the Battn. at 8.30 p.m.	
5th "	Received orders at 1 a.m. for A & D Cos. to be temporarily attached to 2nd Divn. for more work at PONT FIXE and for repairing roads. A & B Cos. marched off at 6.30 a.m. on BETHUNE and BEUVRY to PONT FIXE where they were employed until 11 p.m. Three Cos. billeted in BEUVRY for the night.	
6th February.	"Lieut. P.W. JOHNSON joined at 9 a.m. with 30 N.C.O.'s and men. A & D Cos. rejoined the Battn. at 12.0 (noon).	[signature] Capt.

Army Form C. 2118.

WAR DIARY
or
INTELLIGENCE SUMMARY.
(Erase heading not required.)

Instructions regarding War Diaries and Intelligence Summaries are contained in F. S. Regs., Part II. and the Staff Manual respectively. Title pages will be prepared in manuscript.

Hour, Date, Place	Summary of Events and Information	Remarks and references to Appendices
CHOQUES.		
7th February	Divine Service in Brewery at 10.30 a.m. Lieut F. GODFREY and 67 3COs & men joined the Battn at 2 p.m. 66 3COs and men in addition joined later in the day. The above with the 70 3COs and men who joined yesterday are posted to a new "C" Company under Captain P.C. ESDAILE.	
8th February	Ordinary Routine	
9th "	Captain I.C. ESDAILE and 100 3COs and men proceeded to BEUVRY to join A.O. Coy for work on defences under the 2nd Divn. Capt M.L. HEATH placed in command of the Detachment of three Companies. Captain H.W. STERNHOUSE left the Battn to take up duty as G.S.O.3 to 4th Corps. Ordinary Routine. Casualties:- 1 man severely wounded.	Strength of Battn:- 26 Officers, 33 Sgts, 24 Cpls, 43 L/Cs, 1 Dr and 548 men with 2 Officers and 23 Other ranks attached.
10th "	Ordinary Routine.	
11th "	—	
12th "	—	
13th "	—	
14th "	Divine Service in the Brewery at 10.30 a.m.	

J.O.B. Capt

Army Form C. 2118.

WAR DIARY
or
INTELLIGENCE SUMMARY.
(Erase heading not required.)

Hour, Date, Place	Summary of Events and Information	Remarks and references to Appendices
CHOQUES		
15th February 1915.	Ordinary Routine. Reinforcement of 42 3 C.O's and seven men.	
16th "	" "	
17th "	— — Companies of DEVONS had 3 Casualties — One man died of wounds – 2 slightly wounded.	
18th " " 6.20pm	Ordinary Routine.	
21st " "	Devons arrived in Brewery at 9.30 a.m. Reinforcement of 57 3 C.O. and men arrived.	Strength of Batt. Batt: H. Qrs. 5 Officers 84 other ranks A Co. 5 " 207 " " B Co. 3 " 207 " " C Co. 5 " 208 " " D Co. 4 " 63 " "
22nd " " 6.26pm	Ordinary Routine.	
27th " "	Reinforcement of 63 3 C.O's and men joined at 7 pm and were posted to D Co.	
28th " "	Devons arrive in the Brewery at 9.30 a.m.	

for Capt

I Corps Troops.

WAR DIARY

1st Battalion ROYAL WEST SURREYS

March

1 9 1 5

Attached :- Appendices
XVI to XXI.

WAR DIARY or INTELLIGENCE SUMMARY.

Army Form C. 2118.

(Erase heading not required.)

Instructions regarding War Diaries and Intelligence Summaries are contained in F. S. Regs., Part II. and the Staff Manual respectively. Title pages will be prepared in manuscript.

Hour, Date, Place	Summary of Events and Information	Remarks and references to Appendices
CHOQUES		
1st March 1915	Ordinary Routine	
2nd "	"	
3rd "	50 3 CO's men returned from BEUVRY to own Regt' H.Q.	
4th "	Ordinary Routine	
5th "	54 3 CO's and men returned from BEUVRY to own Regt' H.Q.	
6th "	Ordinary Routine	
	52 3 CO's and men returned from BEUVRY to own Regt' H.Q.	
7th to 8th "	Ordinary Routine	
9th "	177 3 CO's and men returned from BEUVRY to own Regt' H.Q.	
	66 3 CO's and men joined the Batt'n from the Base.	
PONT LEVIS	Paraded at 6.30 a.m. At PONT LEVIS (just N of BETHUNE) at 8 a.m.	Ref. App. XVI(a)
10th "	and start by no 1st Corps Reserve till 7 p.m. Went into billets in area	Vide BETHUNE map 1:100
	immediately N of Canal Regt' H.Q. an luncer W 29 (c)(1d)	
11th and 12th "	Stood by from 8 a.m. till 6.30 p.m. at PONT LEVIS as 1st Corps Reserve	Ref. App. XVI (b)
BETHUNE	Stood by in billets today ready to turn out at half an hours notice	Ref. App. XVII - XVIII
13th "		Ref. App. XIX - XXI
14th "	To be ready to turn out at 2 hours notice in future. Divine Service in	
	field at 11 a.m. About 1 S.O. 3 C.O.'s and men joined the Batt"	

Geo. W. Capt

Army Form C. 2118.

WAR DIARY
or
INTELLIGENCE SUMMARY.
(*Erase heading not required.*)

Instructions regarding War Diaries and Intelligence Summaries are contained in F. S. Regs., Part II. and the Staff Manual respectively. Title pages will be prepared in manuscript.

Hour, Date, Place	Summary of Events and Information	Remarks and references to Appendices
BETHUNE.		
15th March to 21st March	Ordinary Routine	
22" " to 29" "	" "	9" to Capt
30" " to 31" "	" "	

SECRET.   App XVI(a)   Copy No. 13.

To be there 6 am.

1st CORPS OPERATION ORDER No. 70.

9th March, 1915.

1. The British Expeditionary Force will resume the offensive tomorrow (10th).
   The 4th and Indian Corps will force the enemy about NEUVE CHAPELLE and drive back any hostile forces from the line AUBERS - LIGNY LE GRAND with the object of cutting off the enemy's troops now holding the front between NEUVE CHAPELLE and LA BASSEE.
   The 1st Corps will assault the enemy's lines east of GIVENCHY.

2. The 2nd Division will carry out the assault from GIVENCHY in accordance with special instructions which have been issued to G.O.C.

3. The following additional artillery has been placed at disposal of 2nd Division to support this attack :-
   1 F.A. Brigade (2 batteries 18 prs.) from 1st Division.
   44th Brigade, R.F.A. (Hows.)
   26th and 35th Heavy Batteries, R.G.A.
   1st Siege Battery, R.G.A.
   One 9.2" Howitzer, R.G.A.

4. Hostile batteries north of the line FESTUBERT - RUE DU MARAIS - BEAU PUITS will be engaged by artillery disposed under 1st Army instructions.

5. The General Commanding XXI C.A.F. has agreed that certain batteries of 58th French Division shall support the attack by oblique fire on hostile positions east of CUINCHY and south-east of GIVENCHY, and by engaging hostile batteries south of LA BASSEE. Details to be arranged between 2nd Division and 58th French Division.

6. The artillery will complete such registration as is necessary by 7:30 a.m., at which hour the preliminary bombardment will begin.

7. 1st Division will co-operate by a fire attack along its entire front simultaneously with attacks of 2nd Division and Indian and 4th Corps, and both divisions will take advantage of any weakening or retirement of the enemy in its front by a vigorous offensive towards VIOLAINES and BEAU PUITS.

8. <u>1st Corps Reserve</u>.- 2 Battns. 4th (Guards) Brigade at LE PREOL.
         1st Bn. Queen's Regt. (less 1 company) at road junction map square W.30.c.
   <u>1st Army Reserve</u>.- 2nd Infantry Brigade, LOCON - LES CHOQUAUX.
   These reserves will be assembled in readiness at 8 a.m.

9. <u>Report Centre</u>.- Road junction map square E.4.a. from 7 a.m.

R. Whigham Brig. General.
S.G.S.O., 1st Corps.

Issued at 9 a.m. to :-
   1st Division.
   2nd Division.
   Indian Corps.
   Indian Cavalry Corps.
   XXI C.A.F.
   No. 3 Squadron, R.F.C.

"A" Form. Army Form C. 2121.

MESSAGES AND SIGNALS.

Prefix	Code	m.	Words	Charge	This message is on a/c of:	Recd. at ___ m.
Office of Origin and Service Instructions.			Sent		App XVI Service.	Date ___
			At ___ m.			From ___
			To			By ___
			By		(Signature of "Franking Officer.")	

TO — ~~1st Div~~ Corps Troops
~~2nd Div~~

Sender's Number: GA.21. Day of Month: 10. In reply to Number: AAA

The 4th and Indian Corps captured NEUVE CHAPELLE today and at 6 pm were still making progress towards PIETRE and the BOIS de BIEZ about 500 prisoners were taken aaa The offensive of the 2nd Div played its part in holding the enemy in front of LA BASSEE aaa. The forward movement of 4th and Indian Corps will be continued tomorrow aaa one battalion 1st Div has been placed under the orders of Meerut Div and will push forward on the right of that division during the attack intervals gaining ground to the South and joining hands with the left of 1st Division in accordance with specific instructions which have been issued

From ___
Place ___
Time ___

The above may be forwarded as now corrected. (Z)

Censor. Signature of Addressor or person authorised to telegraph in his name
*This line should be erased if not required.

"A" Form.   Army Form C. 2121.

MESSAGES AND SIGNALS.

Prefix	Code	m.	Words	Charge		This message is on a/c of:	Recd. at	m.
Office of Origin and Service Instructions.			Sent			App XVI Service.	Date	
			At	m.			From	
			To					
			By			(Signature of "Franking Officer.")	By	

TO { (2)

Sender's Number	Day of Month	In reply to Number	AAA

To 1st Div aaa 1st Div will be prepared to join hands with this Battalion as the movement progresses aaa 2nd Div will continue its vigorous offensive against the enemy E of GIVENCHY in accordance with special instructions issued herewith aaa Corps Reserve 2nd Inf Bde about LOCON and 1st Bn Queens Regt in position as today aaa These reserves are in readiness & am aaa Report Centre no junction E.L.I.A. from your Acknowledge

From 1st Corps
Place
Time 8-30 pm

The above may be forwarded as now corrected. (Z)
Censor. Signature of Addressee or person authorised to telegraph in his name

*This line should be erased if not required.

"A" Form. Army Form C. 2121.
MESSAGES AND SIGNALS.

TO: ~~1st Divn~~ ~~2nd Divn~~ Corps Troops ~~Indian Corps~~ ~~Indian Army Corps~~

On a/c of: App XVII Service.

Sender's Number	Day of Month	In reply to Number	
GA 24	11th		AAA

The attack of Indian and 4th Corps on our left has made further progress today aaa the statements of prisoners captured at NEUVE CHAPELLE all agree that no troops are opposed to us N of the Canal other than seventh Corps the right of which extends a little beyond BAS MAISNIL aaa First Corps will continue in active observation of the enemy in its front ready to take advantage of any weakening of the hostile line aaa the enemy will be engaged by rifle and machine gun fire during the night and after daylight aaa Facing orders for a definite bombardment with a view to an infantry assault artillery fire will be restricted to slow fire

"A" Form.   Army Form C. 2121.
MESSAGES AND SIGNALS.   No. of Message _____

| Prefix ___ Code ___ m. | Words. | Charge. | This message is on a/c of: | Recd. at ___ m. |
| Office of Origin and Service Instructions. | Sent At ___ m. To ___ By ___ | | App XVII Service. (Signature of "Franking Officer.") | Date ___ From ___ By ___ |

TO { (2)

| Sender's Number | Day of Month | In reply to Number | AAA |

with occasional bursts of a few rounds at more rapid rate aaa The 1st Div will be on the alert to join in any forward movement by BAREILLY B'de aaa Army Reserve is Trg area Corps Reserve 6 Inf B'de aa No Queen's Regt aaa This Div to be in position to & am Recces Hurt as today aaa 2nd Div will reinforce positions of C B'de on Right Centre E.4 a.m. from — I am addressing 1st & 2nd Army Corps Indian repeated Indian & India Cavy Corps aaa Acknowledge

From M. Corps
Place
Time

The above may be forwarded as now corrected. (Z)   Rawlinson LGnl
Censor.   Signature of Addressor or person authorised to telegraph in his name

* This line should be erased if not required.
(24473). M.R.Co., Ltd. Wt.W4843/541. 50,000. 9/14. Forms C2121/10.

O.C.
1st Queens Regt.
  "For your information."

        JH Burn-Lindon.
                    Major
11/3/15.   Comdt. 1st Corps

"A" Form.
MESSAGES AND SIGNALS.

Army Form C. 2121.
No. of Message 45

Prefix	Code	m.	Words.	Charge.		
Office of Origin and Service Instructions.					This message is on a/c of:	Recd. at
			Sent		App XVIII Service.	Date
			At	m.		From
			To		(Signature of "Franking Officer.")	By
			By			

TO { ~~1st~~ ~~2nd~~ 1st Queens Regt

Sender's Number	Day of Month	In reply to Number	
GA.31	Twelfth		AAA

The attacks of Indians and 4th Corps today have been very successful and the enemy has shown signs of demoralization aaa troops in front line must exercise great vigilance to discover the first signs of a withdrawal from hostile trenches aaa patrols must be pushed forward right up to the enemy line and every effort made to enter his trenches aaa bursts of rifle + machine gun must be opened at intervals particularly just before ~~daylight~~ and after daylight aaa all reserves are to be ready to move ~~to at~~ at 30 minutes notice

Acknowledge

From: 1st Corps
Place:
Time: 6.30 pm

The above may be forwarded as now corrected. (Z)

Censor. Signature of Addressee or person authorised to telegraph in his name

* This line should be erased if not required.

(24473). M.R.Co.,Ltd. Wt.W4243/541. 50,000. 9/14. Forms C2121/10.

"A" Form.
Army Form C. 2121.

MESSAGES AND SIGNALS.

No. of Message ____

Prefix ____ Code ____ m.	Words	Charge	This message is on a/c of:	Recd. at ____ m.
Office of Origin and Service Instructions.	Sent		App XIX Service.	Date ____
	At ____ m.			From ____
	To			By ____
	By		(Signature of "Franking Officer.")	

TO: 1st BN QUEENS

Sender's Number	Day of Month	In reply to Number	
1G138	13		AAA

Following from Indian Corps 7.15am begins situation on Indian Corps front quiet aaa Estimate of German dead SE of NEUVE CHAPELLE about 2000 aaa There appears to be a new trench heavily sandbagged on West side of LA BASSÉE road and parallel to it which is meant to enfilade an advance on BOIS DU BIEZ aaa At 3.30am noise of men and carts heard about road junction S11a ends. Air reconnaissance this morning showed one train steam up DON STN facing East centre carriages were blown up by bomb aaa large building first S of DON STN containing about one battalion infantry forming up on parade aaa House close to this bombed aaa Otherwise area behind first corps clear

From: 1st CORPS
Place:
Time: 1 pm

Gort Capt.

"A" Form. Army Form C. 2121.
MESSAGES AND SIGNALS.

TO: ... 1st Bn Queen's

Sender's Number	Day of Month	In reply to Number	AAA
19/40	13		

Message from First Army begins this morning attack by 7th Division was checked by hostile artillery from supposed bodies of BIETRE and material advance beyond the was held last night was followed on other parts of line no advance has been attempted aaa Hostile counter attack from SW on BIEZ about 3.12pm this afternoon died away under artillery fire aaa addressed First and Second Div

From: 1st CORPS
Time: 4.30pm

Gort Capt.

"A" Form.

MESSAGES AND SIGNALS.

No. of Message ___

Prefix ___ Code ___ Words. ___ Charge. ___
Office of Origin and Service Instructions.

This message is on a/c of:

Recd. at ___ m.
Date ___
Service ___ From ___
(Signature of "Franking Officer") By ___

Sent At ___ m. To ___ By ___

[ARMY TELEGRAPHS stamp 13.VI.15]

TO: 1st Queens Regt

Sender's Number: GA35
Day of Month: 13th
In reply to Number:
AAA

A hostile counter-attack on the forward position of the Indian Corps W of the Bois de Biez was repulsed ___ this afternoon aaa patrols must again be pushed forward tonight to reconnoitre the enemy's posn and information is particularly required as to the state of the ground between the opposing lines and the nature and depth of the enemy's wire entanglements aaa Report to CHOCQUES till further orders aaa Acknowledge

From: 1st Corps
Place:
Time: 5.10 pm

The above may be forwarded as now corrected. (Z)

Censor. Signature of Addressor or person authorised to telegraph in his name

* This line should be erased if not required.
(24473). M.R.Co.,Ltd. Wt.W4&43/541. 50,000. 9/14. Forms C2121/10.

I Corps Troops.

WAR DIARY

1st BATTN. THE QUEEN'S (ROYAL WEST SURREY REGIMENT).

A P R I L

1 9 1 5

Army Form C. 2118.

WAR DIARY
or
INTELLIGENCE SUMMARY.
(Erase heading not required.)

Instructions regarding War Diaries and Intelligence Summaries are contained in F. S. Regs., Part II. and the Staff Manual respectively. Title pages will be prepared in manuscript.

Hour, Date, Place	Summary of Events and Information	Remarks and references to Appendices
BETHUNE.		
1st April	Ordinary Routine.	
2nd "	Received order to be ready to move at short notice from 5 a.m.	
	Tomorrow	
3rd "	Received ordinary routine after 10 a.m.	
4th " to 8th April	Ordinary routine. Route marches, company training and drill etc.	
9th "	Evacuated billets at 9.45 a.m. owing to a readjustment of areas	
	Marched via GONNEHEM to LE HAMEL (N of GONNEHEM)	
LE HAMEL.		
10th April to 24th April	Ordinary Routine	
25th April	Reinforcement of 1 Sergt and 59 Privates joined the Batt'n	
26th " 6.30 p.m	Ordinary Routine	

Jones Capt

I Corps Troops.

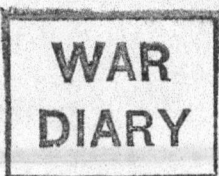

1st BATTN. THE QUEEN'S (ROYAL WEST SURREY REGIMENT).

M A Y

1 9 1 5

Appendices
XXII & XXIII.

WAR DIARY or INTELLIGENCE SUMMARY.

(Erase heading not required.)

Army Form C. 2118.

Hour, Date, Place	Summary of Events and Information	Remarks and references to Appendices
LE HAMEL.		
1st May to 5th May.	Ordinary Routine.	
6th May	Confidential orders of operations received as well as verbal instructions from 1st Corps. The Batt. M. Gun Det. is placed at disposal of 6th Guards Bde for same. O.C. to be sent to Reserve at LOCON under order of A.P.M. 1st Corps. B.C.O. undertaking the same duties at BETHUNE. Detachment of 113 men 1 D.S.O. 6 L/Cpls H.Qrs. Remainder of D.C's. Left at CHOCQUES with 1 L/Cpl at M.O.Qrs. Remainder of D.C's. with A.C.O and Batt. H.Qrs. to move into E. BETHUNE by 5 a.m. on Saturday May 8th and be disposed of 9 O.C. MAC for operations.	
7th May.	Captain Pain and the Machine Gun detachment proceeded to CUINCHY at 7 a.m. Captain Sobolde with 5 O.R's proceeded to LOCON at 1 p.m. The remr. of the remainder of the Batt. was postponed until further orders at 7 p.m.	Ref. App. XXII
8th May.	A draft of 50 O.R's and men arrived at 2 p.m. Recvd. orders at 8:30 p.m. to move at 3:20 a.m. tomorrow as previously instructed.	Jrys Capt

WAR DIARY or INTELLIGENCE SUMMARY.

(Erase heading not required.)

Army Form C. 2118.

Instructions regarding War Diaries and Intelligence Summaries are contained in F. S. Regs., Part II. and the Staff Manual respectively. Title pages will be prepared in manuscript.

Hour, Date, Place	Summary of Events and Information	Remarks and references to Appendices
N.E. BETHUNE. 9th May	Marched off from LE HAMEL at 3.20 a.m. and reached our forming up NE BETHUNE by 5 a.m. Bombardment commenced at 5 a.m. and 1st Divn attacked at 5.40 a.m.	
	The Battn stood by all day under orders to move at half an hours notice.	
10th May	B and C Companies reported the Battn ready by 12.0 noon. At 5 p.m. received orders to go into Billets at VENDIN LEZ BETHUNE.	
VENDIN LEZ BETHUNE. 11th May	Ordinary Routine	
12th "	— Several Officers of the 2nd Battn came over during the afternoon (2nd Battn at ESSARS)	
13th "	Ordinary Routine	
14th "	Received Secret orders that operations would commence at 2 a.m. tomorrow. The 2nd & 7th Divns are to carry out the attack. The Battn is to be under orders of G.O.C. 2nd Corps ready to move at one hours notice.	Ref App XXIII
15th "	Stood by till 12.0 noon when fresh instructions were received that the attack had been postponed. At 5 p.m. C.O. was despatched to BETHUNE to escort details with prisoners escorting from 1st Corps	

Army Form C. 2118.

WAR DIARY
or
INTELLIGENCE SUMMARY.
(Erase heading not required.)

Instructions regarding War Diaries and Intelligence Summaries are contained in F. S. Regs., Part II. and the Staff Manual respectively. Title pages will be prepared in manuscript.

Hour, Date, Place	Summary of Events and Information	Remarks and references to Appendices
N.E BETHUNE		
16th May	The Batt" (less one company) marched off from VENDIN at 3.30am and went into Billets at N.E. BETHUNE. The attack of 3rd & 7th Divn took place as previously arranged. Stood by all day at one hour notice to move.	
17th "	Stood by all day at one hour notice to move. A Co" proceeded to LOCON for escort duty with prisoners at 3 p.m.	
18th "	Band D Co" pleasant dropped of 2nd Div" and marched off at 11.30am to LE TOURET. Lieut P.W. JOHNSON and 9 wounds drawing the night 18/19. 7 other ranks wounded.	Employed in clearing battlefield for 2nd Divn three successive nights.
" "	A Company rejoined from LOCON at 6 p.m. C Co" rejoined from BETHUNE at 9 p.m.	
19 "		
20th "	One man died of wounds and two men killed & 3 wounded.	Capt P.C. ESDAILE and Capt R.L.J. Heath proceeded to join the 2nd Batt" by order of G.H.Q.
21st "	B & D Companies rejoined Batt: H.Q"rs at 6 a.m. Order to stand by at 1 hours notice cancelled at 2 p.m.	
22nd "	Present orders at 10 p m. to stand by at 1 hour notice.	Received thanks of G.O.C 1st Divn & G.O.C 1st Corps for work carried out by Bund D Coys from 18/21 inst.
23rd "	Order to stand by cancelled at 11 a.m & at any notice received	
24th "	Italy declared war upon Austria. Ordinary Routine.	J.M.S Capt

Army Form C. 2118.

WAR DIARY
or
INTELLIGENCE SUMMARY.
(Erase heading not required.)

Instructions regarding War Diaries and Intelligence Summaries are contained in F. S. Regs., Part II. and the Staff Manual respectively. Title pages will be prepared in manuscript.

Hour, Date, Place	Summary of Events and Information	Remarks and references to Appendices
N.E. BETHUNE.		
25th May.	Battn ordered to stand by at 2 an hrs notice from 6 p.m. today.	Ref. Appx XXIV
	Ready for an attack by London Divn & Canadian Divn N of GIVENCHY. 2 hrs notice to stand by increased	
26" "	At 6 p.m. ordered within 6 place 2 Companies at disposal of 47" Divn	to 2 hrs.
	for collecting wounded and burying dead. A & C Coys under Captain	Capt T. NEEDING and Lieut
	Tarnell proceeded to GIVENCHY and worked all night.	E.D. DREW joined the Battn
27." "	A & C Coys returned to Billets at 10 a.m. "Lieut J.B. CLOSE	
	wounded. 1 man killed and five men wounded.	
	B & D Coys placed at disposal of 47" Divn to carry on the work	
	from 8 p.m. tonight under Captain M.J. HEATH.	
28." "	B & D Coys returned to Billets at 11 a.m. Order to stand by at 2 hrs	"Lieut A.C. ARMITAGE joined
	notice cancelled at 12.30 (noon)	the Battn at 6 p.m.
29." "	Ordinary Routine	
30 & 31st	Received orders at 9 p.m. 31st to move to MARLES LES	
	MINES tomorrow afternoon	

Jas Capt.

APPENDICES XXII & XXIII.

App XXII

S E C R E T.

Copy No. 4

1st CORPS OPERATION ORDER No. 79.

7th May, 1915.

Reference maps (1/40,000 (BETHUNE).
(1/20,000 "B" Series, Sheets 36 S.W. & 36c N.W.
(1/10,000

1. The 1st Army will advance tomorrow with the object of breaking through the enemy's line and gaining the LA BASSEE - LILLE road between LA BASSEE and FOURNES.
   Its further advance will be directed on the line BAUVIN - DON.
   Two Cavalry Corps and three Divisions are being held in readiness as a General Reserve under the orders of the Field Marshal Commanding-in-Chief to exploit any success.

2. The 1st Corps is to attack from the RUE DU BOIS and advance on RUE DU MARAIS - ILLIES, maintaining its right at GIVENCHY and CUINCHY.

3. The Indian Corps is to attack on the left of the 1st Corps and is to capture the DISTILLERY and the FERME DU BIEZ. Its subsequent advance will be directed on LIGNY-LE-GRAND - LA CLIQUETERIE FARM.
   The road FERME DU BIEZ - LIGNY-LE-PETIT - LIGNY-LE-GRAND is assigned to the Indian Corps.

4. The 1st Division will attack from its breastworks in front of the RUE DU BOIS.
   Its first objectives are :-
   Hostile trenches P.8. - P.10., the road junction P.15., and the road thence to LA TOURELLE.
   Its subsequent advance will be directed on RUE DU MARAIS - LORGIES a defensive flank being organized from "THE ORCHARD" (P.4.), by LA QUINQUE to RUE DU MARAIS.
   Touch will be maintained with the Indian Corps throughout.

5. The infantry under G.O.C. London Division holding the defensive front north of FESTUBERT will be prepared to relieve the infantry of the 1st Division at "THE ORCHARD (P.4), LA QUINQUE RUE, and RUE DU MARAIS, when those points have been secured, and to take advantage of any weakening of the enemy about the RUE d'OUVERT to occupy that locality.

6. The 2nd Division (less 4th Guards Brigade), with Motor Machine Gun Battery attached, will be in Corps Reserve in the area LOISNE - LE TOURET - LE HAMEL in readiness to continue the advance. The troops of 1st Division must be clear of above area by 3:30 a.m.

7. The 5th London Brigade will be in 1st Army Reserve, about ESSARS and LES CHOQUAUX, from 5 a.m.

8. The 1st Bn. Queen's Regt (less two companies) will be under the direct orders of the Corps Commander north of BETHUNE.

9. The artillery will complete such registration as may be necessary by 5 a.m., at which hour the preliminary bombardment will begin in accordance with special instructions already issued as to times and objectives.
   G.O.C. London Division will arrange for wire cutting batteries and machine guns to open fire on enemy's wire opposite FESTUBERT and CUINCHY at 4:45 a.m.

10. At 5:40 a.m. the infantry of the 1st Division will assault. The troops under G.O.C. London Division will at the same time open a vigorous fire attack along their entire front.

11. Advanced 1st Corps will be established at W.30.a.7.8. at 4 p.m. today.

                                            RWhigham Brig. General.

                                        General Staff, 1st Corps.

Issued at 11:30 a.m. to :-

    1st Division.
    2nd Division.
    London Division.
    1st Bn. Queen's Regt.

    No. 1 Group, H.A.R.
    R.F.C.
    Indian Corps.
    4th Corps.   For information.
    Indian Cav. Corps.
    XXI O.A.F.
    1st Army.

S E C R E T.   App XXIII   Copy No. 6

1st CORPS OPERATION ORDER No. 83.

14th May, 1915.

Reference maps   (1/10,000.
                     (1/40,000

1. The 1st Army will resume its offensive tonight.

2. Its object is to press forward to VIOLAINES and BEAU PUITS, establishing a defensive flank on the LA BASSEE - ESTAIRES road on the left and maintaining the right at GIVENCHY.

3. The main attack will be carried out by the 1st and Indian Corps.

4. The first objective is the general line of the road FESTUBERT - LA QUINQUE RUE - LA TOURELLE - PORT ARTHUR. This position is to be consolidated when won.

5. The task of the 1st Corps (2nd and 7th Divisions) is to secure the line of the road FESTUBERT - LA TOURELLE from Points M.3. to R.13.

6. The Indian Corps is to assault the German front system of trenches between the ditches running S.S.E. to N.N.W. through Points V.5. and V.6., secure the German second line breastwork and Point V.6., and establish a flank at this point connecting with our present line.

    This assault is to be delivered at 11:30 p.m. tonight simultaneously with that of 2nd Division.

    As opportunity offers the Indian Corps will subsequently attack outwards towards the line Points V.5.E. - V.6.E. - 59, and having secured that, will push on and secure the road from PORT ARTHUR to LA TOURELLE, as the attack of the 2nd Division progresses.

7. To carry out the task of the 1st Corps :-
   (a) The 2nd Division will assault the German front system of trenches between Point R.1. and the right of the Indian Corps and secure the line R.1. - R.3. - R.5. - R.7.- V.4. under cover of darkness.

        This assault will be delivered at 11:30 p.m. tonight in close touch with the assault of the Indian Corps.

        At 3:15 a.m. tomorrow the 2nd Division will continue to press its attack simultaneously with that of the 7th Division and secure the FERME COUR d'AVOUE AND the line of the FESTUBERT - LA TOURELLE road from Points P.14. to R.13. both inclusive.

   (b) The 7th Division will assault the German position on the front Points N.1. - P.5. at 3:15 a.m. tomorrow.

        First objective:- the enemy's front system of trenches.
        Second objective:- the line of the road from Points M.3. to P.14 at which point close touch is to be established with 2nd Division.

8. Under the direction of the Divisional Commanders concerned, a deliberate bombardment of the enemy's positions will be maintained throughout today and tonight up to the hours fixed respectively for the assaults of 2nd and 7th Divisions, in accordance with instructions already issued. Fire will then be lifted clear of the actual portions of the hostile line to be assaulted.

The

Sheet 2.

The 1st Group, H.A.R., will also take part in this bombardment in accordance with a programme arranged under the supervision of the M.G.R.A., 1st Army, which has been communicated to divisions.

9. (a) The 4th (Guards) Brigade will form the Corps Reserve in readiness to move at short notice from 11:30 p.m. tonight.
(b) The 1st Bn. Queen's Regt. will be under the direct orders of the Corps Commander in its billets and in readiness to move at one hours notice from 3 a.m. tomorrow. Horses of the baggage and supply wagons of this battalion need not be harnessed.

R. Whigham, Brig. General.
General Staff, 1st Corps.

Issued at 1 p.m. to :-

2nd Division.
7th Division.
Barter's Force.
No. 3 Squadron, R.F.C.
1st Group, H.A.R.
1st Bn. Queen's Regt.
Indian Corps.

I Corps Troops.

WAR DIARY

1st BATTN. THE QUEEN'S (ROYAL WEST SURREY REGIMENT).

J U N E

1 9 1 5

WAR DIARY or INTELLIGENCE SUMMARY.

Army Form C. 2118.

Instructions regarding War Diaries and Intelligence Summaries are contained in F. S. Regs., Part II. and the Staff Manual respectively. Title pages will be prepared in manuscript.

(Erase heading not required.)

Hour, Date, Place	Summary of Events and Information	Remarks and references to Appendices
MARLES LES MINES.		
1st June 1915.	Paraded at 2 p.m. and marched to MARLES LES MINES arriving there at 5.0 p.m. and went into billets in W. end of village	
2nd "	Ordinary Routine	
3rd "	Mounted control posts (1 Officer 2 NCO's 15 men) to control traffic	
4th & 5th "	Ordinary Routine.	
6th "	2 Officers and 2 NCO's sent to 29th & 7th 6th R.E. for instruction in Tent-throwing.	
7th & 8th "	Ordinary Routine	
9th "	Major J.K.N. VERSTURME-BUNBURY joined the Battn. on taking command of D Coy. Major Coffs posted to Battn. Captn. A. HEATH ordered to proceed to 2nd Battn. to take command	Officers Commanding Companies:— A Coy. Capt. G.B. PARNELL B " { 2nd Lieut W.L.J. NICHOLAS (Acting) { 2nd Lieut C.B. BROOKE C " Capt. T. WESSING D " Major J.K.N. BUNBURY
10th "	Parties of 1 NCO and 3 men of Regt. Signalling attached to the 2nd and 4th Divn respectively for instruction in Telephone work.	
	Capt. M.G. HEATH proceeded to 2nd Battn	
11th & 12th "	Ordinary Routine	
13th "	Major L.M. CROFTS and 2nd Lieut H.W. GOLDBERG joined the Battn.	2nd Lieut

WAR DIARY
or
INTELLIGENCE SUMMARY.
(Erase heading not required.)

Army Form C. 2118.

Instructions regarding War Diaries and Intelligence Summaries are contained in F. S. Regs., Part II. and the Staff Manual respectively. Title pages will be prepared in manuscript.

Hour, Date, Place	Summary of Events and Information	Remarks and references to Appendices
MARLES LES MINES.		
14th June to 23rd June	Ordinary Routine. Lieut R STUFFIELD joined at the 17th of June.	Treather + st Coldrest out camp 7 days on June 22nd
24th	Received orders to clear up on billets to the N end of MARLES. A B.C. evacuated their billets. R MUNSTER FUSILIERS occupied the area evacuated by us.	
25th	Changed Batt⁹ H⁴ Qrs to W end of village as 1ˢᵗ Divⁿ H.Qrs are taking over our Batt⁹ H.Q. Received orders at 6.p.m. that Batt⁹ is to move to BEUVRY (2½ miles SE of BETHUNE) and to be employed in digging advanced 2nd Line entrenchments in the CAMBRIN area.	
BEUVRY		
26th	Batt⁹ moved into billets in the western part of BEUVRY	
27th to 30th	A.B.+ C. Companies detailed out working parties at CAMBRIN and NOYELLES, worked in two reliefs from 8 a.m. to 5 p.m.	Whilst at "H. Colebrook returned from Sirsh on the 30th

Jas Capt

5th Infantry Brigade.

2nd Division.

(Battn. was I Corps Troops
1st-20th July. Joined
Bde. 21st July)

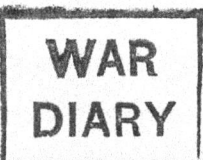

1st BATTN. THE QUEEN'S (ROYAL WEST SURREY REGIMENT).

J U L Y

1 9 1 5

WAR DIARY or INTELLIGENCE SUMMARY.

Army Form C. 2118.

(Erase heading not required.)

Instructions regarding War Diaries and Intelligence Summaries are contained in F. S. Regs., Part II. and the Staff Manual respectively. Title pages will be prepared in manuscript.

Hour, Date, Place	Summary of Events and Information	Remarks and references to Appendices
BEUVRY.		
1st July, 1915.	Working parties of A B C Companies employed in digging 2nd line.	
2nd to 4th July	Entrenchments under orders of 1st Corps.	
5th July	- ditto -	
6th to 10th July	A B & C Co's working under 2nd Div'n from this date, improving defences in the GUINCHY - GINCHY area.	2nd Lieut C.D.M. FOWLER joined the Batt'n
11th July	Usual work.	
12th "	Rest day. Companies employed in cleaning up. Work under 2nd Div'n resumed. 3º/10721 Pte STEPNEY accidentally wounded or killed by another. Casualty:- One man wounded.	The Secretary of State for War paid a visit to the 1st Army H.Q. in July 8th and a group of known was made by the Div'n
13th "	Usual work.	
14th " & 17th July	Usual work.	11 Officers at AIRÉ under 2nd Lt H.NICHOLS
18th "	Rest day. Received wire that the Batt'n in 6th hill in readiness to join the 5th Batt'n R INNISKILL'G FUSILIERS who go to the 3rd Army.	2nd Lieut C.D.M. FOWLER promoted Lieutenant 12-4-15
19th July - 20th July	Ordinary Routine.	
BÉTHUNE		
21st July	The Coll: came under orders of 5th Inf.Bd. from 8 AM today. 2nd Lieut A.C. ARMITAGE and one man accidentally killed and 2nd Lieut J. B. GOLDBERG	Jno. Capt. MP

WAR DIARY or INTELLIGENCE SUMMARY.

Army Form C. 2118.

(Erase heading not required.)

Hour, Date, Place	Summary of Events and Information	Remarks and references to Appendices
BETHUNE		
21st July (continued)	wounded by explosion of BATTIS Hand bomb while practising	"B" Company and Pte PARSONS Buried in BEUVRY cemetery
	The Batt moved into BETHUNE at 5.15pm and billeted in the Tobacco Factory.	
22nd July	Ordinary Routine. Enemy shelled an area at 4.15 p.m. No casualties.	
23rd "	"A" Coy. of Batt" visited trenches at CUINCHY which are to be taken over by Batt" on the 25th of July.	
24th " TRENCHES (CUINCHY)	Enemy shelled an area at 4.0 p.m. No Casualties. 1 Man wounded.	
25th "	Crossed at 7.45 A.M. and marched to CUINCHY. Relief of OXFORDS completed by 12.0 (noon). Quiet day. Casualties 1 Man wounded.	
26th "	Quiet day. Casualties 2nd Lieut G.B. COLEBROOK 2 Men killed & 3 Men wounded. "A" COLEBROOK & Pte HOARE buried at A 20 b.6.8. N.N.W.	
27th "	Quiet day.	
	side of town. (Bethune to-day)	
28th "	Enemy shelled left front b" at Brickstacks. Casualties nil.	"2nd Lt H. BATTISCOMBE joined the Batt."
29th "	Enemy bombarded of GLASGOW 1/4 hr from support points at CUINCHY and CAMBRIN, C Coy and ½ D Coy drawn in their places.	
	Relief of remainder of Batt" by OXFORDS completed by 5.0pm. The Batt" H Q in were shelled during the relief. Casualties. 1 Man killed & 7 wounded. The Batt" went into billets at ANNEQUIN.	

Army Form C. 2118.

WAR DIARY
or
INTELLIGENCE SUMMARY.
(Erase heading not required.)

Instructions regarding War Diaries and Intelligence Summaries are contained in F. S. Regs., Part II. and the Staff Manual respectively. Title pages will be prepared in manuscript.

Hour, Date, Place	Summary of Events and Information	Remarks and references to Appendices
ANNEQUIN.		
30th July.	Ordinary Routine.	
31st " "	" "	2Lieut J. R. DREW joined the Battn.

5th Infantry Brigade.
2nd Division.

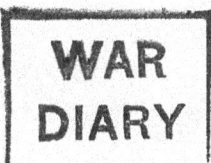

1st BATTN. THE QUEEN'S (ROYAL WEST SURREY REGIMENT).

A U G U S T

1 9 1 5

Army Form C. 2118.

WAR DIARY
or
INTELLIGENCE SUMMARY.
(Erase heading not required.)

Instructions regarding War Diaries and Intelligence Summaries are contained in F.S. Regs., Part II. and the Staff Manual respectively. Title pages will be prepared in manuscript.

Hour, Date, Place	Summary of Events and Information	Remarks and references to Appendices
ANNEQUIN		
1st August	Draft of 51 joined under Lieut R.C. JOYNSON-HICKS.	
2nd CUINCHY (Trenches)	The Batt'n relieved the OXFORD L.I. by 2 p.m. in CUINCHY section	
3rd "	Ordinary Routine in Trenches. Casualties Nil.	
4th "	" " " " " "	
5th "	" " Casualties 6 wounded	
6th "	" " " 1 wounded	
7th "	Batt'n relieved by 66th Rifles (6th & 4th) at 7 p.m. Casualties 3 killed 3 wounded	
VENDIN LES BETHUNE.		
8th "	Ordinary Routine.	Capt. A.W.H. Paun should have
9th to 14th "	" "	returned from leave, but remained
15th Aug. LE QUESNOY	Batt'n moved to LE QUESNOY and went into billets.	in England on Medical Certificate.
16. Aug	Ordinary Routine. Casualties Nil.	
17th " and 18th "	" " " "	
	a month's	
	for drafts in training staff for the 18th	
19 "	Officers & TT Batt'n went round Trenches in B2 Sector at GIVENCHY	
	with a view to taking over from OXFORDS on the 20th. Working party of	
	B 16t employed in defence of GIVENCHY were shelled.	
	Casualties 4 killed & 2 wounded.	

WAR DIARY or INTELLIGENCE SUMMARY.

Army Form C. 2118.

Hour, Date, Place	Summary of Events and Information	Remarks and references to Appendices
S..B 2 GIVENCHY (in trenches)		
20th August	Draft of 25 joined the Batt" at 11 a.m. The Batt" relieved the 2/Oxfords between 2 p.m. and 5 p.m. in sector B 2 - N of GIVENCHY. Enemy's trenches very close here, average of 300-400 yards. Thrown out night firing from Sup: trenches. Casualty 1 Killed.	[scribbled out]
21st "	Quiet morning. Our front line shelled at 2 p.m. till 3.30 p.m. while on Art? shelled Enemy's front line trenches. Casualty 1 wounded. Enemy Replied at 3.30 p.m. and shelled our Support line in SCOTTISH TRENCH. Patrol out every night. No information.	
22nd "	Our Art? shelled enemy at 2 p.m. Enemy retaliated on our front line. Casualties 1 Killed, 1 wounded. Tested 15th Bat? 9 R.F.A. at 10 p.m. and obtained fire in half a minute.	Lt. A.M. ALLAN struck off its strength having proceeded sick to England.
23rd "	Heard of issuing of Russian Flast in the Baltic. A written account, in German, was made out and thrown in a bottle onto the German parapet. Casualties 2 Killed and 5 wounded. Tested 47th Heritage Battery at 11.30 p.m. and obtained fire in 3½ minutes.	2/Lt. W.B. CORSLAKE joined the Batt? Jos Cape
24th "	Relieved by OXFORDS between 11.30 a.m. and 2 p.m. The Batt?	

Army Form C. 2118.

WAR DIARY
or
INTELLIGENCE SUMMARY.
(Erase heading not required.)

Instructions regarding War Diaries and Intelligence Summaries are contained in F.S. Regs., Part II. and the Staff Manual respectively. Title pages will be prepared in manuscript.

Hour, Date, Place	Summary of Events and Information	Remarks and references to Appendices
LE QUESNOY		
24th Aug. (continued)	marched back by Platoons and billetted in LE QUESNOY. Casualties 1 wounded.	
25th "	Ordinary Routine. One Company on Fatigue at Gonnehem.	
26th " & 27th "	— ditto —	
28th "	Bedford (2d Kt R.) relieved the 7th Bn. during afternoon.	
N.E. BETHUNE	Marched to CEMETARY area N.E. BETHUNE & went into Hutts. One man accidentally drowned in Open air Bath Bethune.	
29th "	Church Parade in Bethune Theatre at 11 a.m. The 2nd Batt. at LOCON today and several Officers and men visited them.	
30th & 31st	Ordinary Routine	

5th Infantry Brigade.

2nd Division.

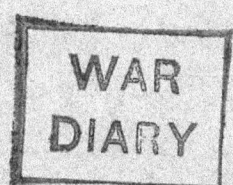

1st BATTN. THE QUEEN'S (ROYAL WEST SURREY REGIMENT).

S E P T E M B E R

1 9 1 5

Army Form C. 2118.

WAR DIARY
or
INTELLIGENCE SUMMARY.
(Erase heading not required.)

Instructions regarding War Diaries and Intelligence Summaries are contained in F.S. Regs., Part II. and the Staff Manual respectively. Title pages will be prepared in manuscript.

Hour, Date, Place	Summary of Events and Information	Remarks and references to Appendices
N.E. BETHUNE.		
1st Sept.	Ordinary Routine. The Battn. gave a concert from 6.30 to 8.30 pm in the Theatre Bethune.	
2nd "	Ordinary Routine.	
3rd "	5th Battn relieved the 2/1st Batt. during the afternoon. Our Battn. took over from Battn. in B.3 Section (sect 32) in the North of GIVENCHY by 5.30 p.m. Quiet night.	
SECTION B3 GIVENCHY		
4th Sept and 5th "	Ordinary work in the trenches, improving and deepening trenches making dug outs, wiring etc. Trenches etc. Quiet nights.	
6th "	One of our mines was exploded at 5.30 AM, no casualties but our trenches slightly damaged by the explosion. Relieved by orders at 5.30 p.m. and marched back to billets in LE QUESNOY.	
LE QUESNOY		
7th Sept	Ordinary Routine.	
8th "	Battn. relieved Oxfords at 5.30pm in B.3 Section	
Section B.3.	Ordinary work as on the 4th & 5th. 2 Lieut C.W. ELTHAM, Lieut J.R.	
9th "	DREW and 3 other ranks wounded by premature explosion of our PITCHER (double cylinder) bombs.	gas Capt

Army Form C. 2118.

WAR DIARY
or
INTELLIGENCE SUMMARY.
(Erase heading not required.)

Instructions regarding War Diaries and Intelligence
Summaries are contained in F. S. Regs., Part II.
and the Staff Manual respectively. Title pages
will be prepared in manuscript.

Hour, Date, Place	Summary of Events and Information	Remarks and references to Appendices
Bethune B.3.		
Sept 10th	Casualties - One other Rank. Oxfords relieved the Batt: at 5pm and we marched back to billets in LE QUESNOY.	
LE QUESNOY Sept 11th	Ordinary Routine. The Batt: was to have relieved Oxfords in Bethune B.3 at 5 pm tomorrow, but orders cancelled at 9 pm as the 19th B.de are relieving the 5th B.de on the 13th.	
Sept 12th	Ordinary Routine. Divine Service 11.30 a.m in Chateau grounds.	
NE Bethune " 13th	Received orders to move tomorrow to Cemetary Area BETHUNE. Batt: assembled at 4.30 p.m and marched to cemetary area where billets were taken over from Camerouns.	
Sept 14th	Ordinary work including musketry. Bathing & testing of smoke helmets, inspection of rifles etc.	
" 15th	A draft of 18 other ranks joined the Batt: Route march at 2 pm. Ordinary Routine.	
" 16th Bethune B.2. " 17th	Batt: marched off at 3 pm and billeted 14.21 in B2 section. Casualties Nil.	
" 18th	Ordinary work in trenches. Casualties 1 Killed & 5 wounded.	gas Capt

Army Form C. 2118.

WAR DIARY
or
INTELLIGENCE SUMMARY.
(Erase heading not required.)

Hour, Date, Place	Summary of Events and Information	Remarks and references to Appendices
19th Sept.	Relieved by 2/H.L.I. about 6 p.m. and marched back to billets near ESSARS. Casualties 1 wounded	
20.	Aclmon Centre	
21st	"	
Section B2 22nd	Pte Dickinson accidentally shot while talking in the Canal	
LE QUESNOY 30th Sept	Relieved 2/H.L.I. by 3.30 p.m. in Section B.2 near Guinchy. Casualties :- 2 wounded	
Section B.2 26th	Relieved by 2/H.L.I. at 5 p.m. and marched back to billets in LE QUESNOY. Casualties 2 killed and 4 wounded. Took over an advanced frontage in B.2 Section and occupied position of attack however Relief completed at 5 p.m.	Draft of 40 joined
25th	On leading line advanced at 6.7 a.m. and reached the German 3rd line without great opposition. The attack was essentially a complete surprise. The Battⁿ advanced in a frontage of two platoons, D C^o (Major DUNBURY) on the right and B C^o (Capt Booth) on	J.D. Capt

Army Form C. 2118.

WAR DIARY
or
INTELLIGENCE SUMMARY.
(Erase heading not required.)

Hour, Date, Place	Summary of Events and Information	Remarks and references to Appendices
25th Sept (continued).	the left. The advance was necessarily slow to keep behind the creeper. B & D Companies reached the German lines and garrisoned trench with the 2/Oxford L.I. and the 2/H.L.I. on the left and right respectively. The Support Company (C Coy) under Captain Heading held our front line of trenches and, at about 8.15am, two platoons of this Company reinforced B & D Companies, taking up a Supply of Bombs with them. Lieut E D DREW commanded the party. The Enemy developed a strong counter attack on both flanks of the Regt, and our men were unable to reply effectively owing to lack of bombs. At about 9.45am the two and a half companies were obliged to fall back onto our own lines, under a very heavy fire, machine gun fire for the right flank. Casualties:- 2/Lt A W A BRADSHAW, C D M FOWLER and M J B HOWELL killed + missing, 2/Lt F G PLANT wounded and missing, Majr J.K.N DONBURY, Capt C B BROOKE	Days later

Army Form C. 2118.

WAR DIARY
or
INTELLIGENCE SUMMARY.
(Erase heading not required.)

Instructions regarding War Diaries and Intelligence Summaries are contained in F. S. Regs., Part II. and the Staff Manual respectively. Title pages will be prepared in manuscript.

Hour, Date, Place	Summary of Events and Information	Remarks and references to Appendices
25th Sept Cuinchy	Lieut E.D. DREW, Lieut H.P. FOSTER and Lieut R.C. JOHNSON HICKS wounded. Other Ranks 19 killed, 21 missing believed killed, 136 wounded, 80 missing and wounded & missing. 7 Stragglers from 2nd & 3rd Batt of wounds. Total 266 other ranks. The remainder of the day was spent in reorganising the Bns and in collecting wounded, burying dead etc.	
26th Sept LE PREOL	Relieved by H.L.I. at 3.30 p.m. and went back to billets at LE PREOL	Draft of 30 joined
27th " "	Received orders to start to LE PREOL at 4 p.m. ready to reinforce either the CUINCHY or the sector south of the LA BASSEE Road. Returned to billets at 7 p.m. Casualties nil.	Draft of 8 joined
28th Sept	Received orders to be ready to take on trenches at CAMBRIN this afternoon, but order cancelled later. Marched to billets in BEUVRY at 6 p.m. Casualties nil.	Jaa Cape
BEUVRY 29th Sept	Marched to CAMBRIN at 2 p.m. and took over trenches from	

Army Form C. 2118.

WAR DIARY
or
INTELLIGENCE SUMMARY.
(Erase heading not required.)

Hour, Date, Place	Summary of Events and Information	Remarks and references to Appendices
29th Sept (continued) 30th Sept.	The 10th H.L.I. Trenches in a very bad state. Casualties Nil. Cleaning up trenches and collecting & burying dead all day. Major T. WEEDING wounded. Relieved by 12th R.S. at 11pm and marched to billets at BEUVRY, the man of the Batt: did not reach billets until 6 a.m. on the 1st Oct. 2Lieut A.J. CRICHTON and 2Lieut R.E.C. HARLAND joined the Batt:	Jas Capt

5th Infantry Brigade.

2nd Division.

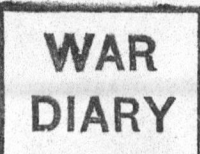

1st BATTN. THE QUEEN'S (ROYAL WEST SURREY REGIMENT).

O C T O B E R

1 9 1 5

Army Form C. 2118.

WAR DIARY
or
INTELLIGENCE SUMMARY.
(Erase heading not required.)

Instructions regarding War Diaries and Intelligence Summaries are contained in F. S. Regs., Part II. and the Staff Manual respectively. Title pages will be prepared in manuscript.

Hour, Date, Place	Summary of Events and Information	Remarks and References to Appendices
October 1st	The Batt'n paraded at 2 p.m. and marched to VERMELLES	
	Short by 1st Bn. Rutlgers first W of VERMELLES until	Capt. J. R. WALPOLE
	8.30 p.m. Went into billets in Emplacements 1 Coy at 10.30 p.m	joined the Batt'n &
	2/Lieut. R. FAULKNER joined the Batt'n	took command of D Coy.
2nd	Remained in reserve all day. Casualties 4 wounded.	
3rd	Relieved by the 3rd Grenade Bn Today. The Batt'n left	
	VERMELLES at 10 a.m. and marched to BETHUNE where	Draft of 100 joined under
	we went into billets in the Tobacco Factory.	2/Lt SS SKEATE and 2/Lt
	Ordinary Routine.	& it PERFECT 3/Kings Own.
4th		
5th	Received orders at 12.0 noon to move to AVELETTE (near	
	HINGES). Reached new billets at 6 p.m.	
AVELETTE.		
6th	Ordinary Routine. Lieuts H.C. WILLIAMS, A.R. ABERCROMBIE,	
	and "Lieut B.M. GREY joined the Batt'n.	
7th	Ordinary Routine including practise in changing line hand grenades.	
8th	Received orders to Stand by at 5.45 p.m. owing to a German attack	
	N.W. of HULLUCH. Order cancelled at 11.30 p.m.	

FAS Capt

Army Form C. 2118.

WAR DIARY
or
INTELLIGENCE SUMMARY.
(Erase heading not required.)

Instructions regarding War Diaries and Intelligence Summaries are contained in F.S. Regs., Part II. and the Staff Manual respectively. Title pages will be prepared in manuscript.

Hour, Date, Place	Summary of Events and Information	Remarks and References to Appendices
AVELETTE 9th Oct.	Manual work. Recvd. orders that the Bn. would take over trenches on the 11th from Grenrs. Bn.	
10th "	Received orders at 8 a.m. that the 5th Bn. would relieve the 21st & party guards 8th Inder. Wounded M/Lt 11th DANNEVIN when Batt. stopped for dinner. Relieved 1/Coldstream guards by 6 p.m. Batt: HQrs Quarry. 6.4.2.5. (50,000)	2 Lieut. J. WHEELER with 14 Caevet Deputies and 1st Grenadier Guards joined.
11th "	Quiet morning. Enemy's aeroplane was brought down in the vicinity of DAILLY LA BOURSE. After an air combat over our lines.	
12th "	Preparation for tomorrows bombing attack. Conference at 5 p.m. 14 Cher at 3.30 p.m.	
13th "	Refused for attack at 10 a.m., placing out bayonet men, bombers, Bayonet groups men, gas helms and working parties in the order that they will advance up NEW TRENCH. 2.0 a/ 1 a.m. when gas & smoke were started. Heavy rifle and machine gun fire was at once opened on our trenches	J.T. Coyle

Forms/C. 2118/11.

WAR DIARY
or
INTELLIGENCE SUMMARY.

(Erase heading not required.)

Army Form C. 2118.

Hour, Date, Place	Summary of Events and Information	Remarks and References to Appendices

In France

13th Oct (continued) — At 2 p.m. the advance up NEW TRENCH was timed to begin. The 13th Bnthn. with head of the attack were held up by rifle and machine gun fire from both flanks and the front, all within a few our own front. The attack was held up for some minutes. Finally 2 Lieut A.R. ABERCROMBIE, 2 Lieut TWEEDIE-SMITH and two 13th Battn Officers with six men advanced up the sap. 2 Lieut A.R. ABERCROMBIE and one man succeeded in reaching the German sap unopposed and advanced up this sap to junction with LITTLE WILLIE. Here they waited for reinforcements. Finally 2/Lt. A penetrated the sap with a runner for supports, seeing himself at the junction of the enemy's trench with LITTLE WILLIE. The orderly was wounded on the way back & no message was delivered. At dusk 2/Lt. A. advanced up LITTLE WILLIE and expended his grenades, placing a German machine gun out of action. He then returned safely to our lines reporting himself.

WAR DIARY
or
INTELLIGENCE SUMMARY.
(Erase heading not required.)

Army Form C. 2118.

Hour, Date, Place	Summary of Events and Information	Remarks and References to Appendices
In the Trenches		
13th Oct. (continued)	Two of our gas cylinders had been left in the trench at Batt: H.Qrs without an knowledge, by R.E. One of these was hit by shell fire during the afternoon and caused considerable annoyance to H. Qrs before the source could be traced. A fresh attack by D. Coy was timed to take place at midnight 13/14, but owing to a shortage of bombs it was not commenced until nearly 5am and then only a short length of the trench (about 30 yds) was gained. Casualties :- "H"c Alt PERFECT 3rd Kings Own Died of wounds. 2nd Lt A. TWEEDIE-SMITH killed. Other Ranks 11 killed 4 # missing and 47 wounded.	2/Lt CARSLAKE led a second bomber attack on western front of HOHENZOLLERN and made a successful advance to corner once during operations, he withdrew after expending his grenades without incurring any casualties.
14th Oct.	Quiet morning. A fresh bombing attack was organised to take place up GUILDFORD TRENCH so as to effect a junction with the 13 & 10 th in HOHENZOLLERN, but this did not mature owing to our relief by OXFORDS at 4 p.m. The Batt came back into Billets at ANNEQUIN. Casualties 1 killed and 3 wounded.	Draft ? 17 other ranks joined. Jas Cape

WAR DIARY
or
INTELLIGENCE SUMMARY.
(Erase heading not required.)

Army Form C. 2118.

Hour, Date, Place	Summary of Events and Information	Remarks and References to Appendices
ANNEQUIN		
15th Oct	Ordinary Routine	
15th "	" A few enemy shells fell near billets.	
	Enemy parties, 120 strong, were found by the Bath" at 6 p.m.	
	11 p.m and 4 a.m the 17th for improving GUILDFORD TRENCH.	
17th Oct.	Quiet day. Working parties of 60 men as above in two reliefs only.	Casualties 2 Other Ranks killed
18th "	Quiet day. Lieut H. E. WILLIAMS accidentally killed by the Enemy when returning to our French during digging operations.	
19th "	Ordinary Routine	
20th "	300 parades provide as all the Batt" was employed in fatigues up at the Tranchée etc.	
21st "	The Batt" paraded at 2 p.m to march to billets at GONNEHEM but this was cancelled while we were on the march owing to the 28th Div" being there. The Batt" went into billets a	
VENDIN	VENDIN instead.	
22nd "	Ordinary Routine.	
23rd "	——— Major S.T. Watson + Capt Hurst + 1, 6th Batt" Came in during afternoon	2nd in Capt

WAR DIARY or INTELLIGENCE SUMMARY

Army Form C. 2118.

Hour, Date, Place	Summary of Events and Information	Remarks and References to Appendices
VENDIN		
24th Oct.	Reinforcement of 50 other ranks joined. This was a particularly good draft, practically all old time serving men who had been wounded, with a good proportion of N.C.O.s.	
25th	Moved we are in trenches from 19.13 to 21.28.d. Ordinary Routine.	
26th		
27th	G.O.C. 2nd Corps was to have inspected us but it was too wet and inspection was postponed. 40th ranks joined together with Capt. F.B. STOREY and 2nd Lieuts J.G. BUCKNER, O.S. FLINN, H.M. RICHARDS, S.W. FARWELL.	
28th	Ordinary Routine. Following joined the Battn: Capt. F.B. STOREY and 2nd Lieuts J.G. BUCKNER, O.S. FLINN, H.M. RICHARDS, and C.W. FARWELL, M.M. & 4 other ranks.	
Trenches 21 CAMBRIN	Batt proceeded at 9 a.m. and marched to CAMBRIN.	
29th	Relief of 1/Middlesex in 21 Sector completed by 11 p.m. Quiet day. Casualties Nil.	Pte J. Taylor
30th	Quiet day. Enemy appear very inactive and appear to be rather H. Battisson's Casualties and other matters. Enemy Snipers were active. Casualties "H" W.O. CANSLAKE wounded. One other rank killed & one wounded.	Lieut A. MUNDYE joined 2nd Lieut H. BATTISSON returned for duty with Trench Mortar Battery.

5th Infantry Brigade.

2nd Division.

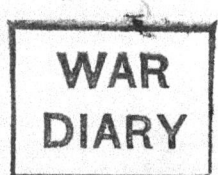

1st BATTN. THE QUEEN'S (ROYAL WEST SURREY REGIMENT).

N O V E M B E R

1 9 1 5

WAR DIARY or INTELLIGENCE SUMMARY.

Army Form C. 2118.

(Erase heading not required.)

Hour, Date, Place	Summary of Events and Information	Remarks and References to Appendices
Oct 21 CAMBRIN		
Nov 1st	Enemy still showing more activity with snipers but no shelling	
	in our sector. Casualties 2 killed 1 wounded	
2nd	Relieved by 2/Ox & Bucks L.I. & 12 o(noon). The Bn	
ANNEZIN	marched back to ANNEZIN and went into billets.	
Nov 3rd	Ordinary Routine. 2nd Lieut L.H. BENNETT and 2 other Ranks	
	joined the Batt.	
" 4th	Ordinary Routine	
" 5th	8 Officers and 400 men proceeded to CAMBRIN for fatigue	
	work at 8 a.m. "Buses supplied by 2nd Div."	
" 6th	Ordinary Routine	
" 7th	Batt. paraded at 10.15 A.M. and marched by Platoons	
" 8th	to ANNEQUIN with one G.M. at CAMBRIN.	
ANNEQUIN	15 Officers and 500 men on carrying work in trenches all	
	day. 2nd Lieut C.W. ROFFE joined. Casualties - 10th Ranks	
" 9th	Ordinary Routine	
" 10th	The Batt. relieved the Glasgow Highrs on 21 Commencing at	

WAR DIARY or INTELLIGENCE SUMMARY

Army Form C. 2118.

(Erase heading not required.)

Instructions regarding War Diaries and Intelligence Summaries are contained in F. S. Regs., Part II. and the Staff Manual respectively. Title pages will be prepared in manuscript.

Hour, Date, Place	Summary of Events and Information	Remarks and References to Appendices
In the Trenches		
Nov 10th (continued)	9 a.m. from CAMBRIN C.H. 12th Div'n in support and 2nd Worcesters (5th Bde) in reinft. Relief completed by 12.0 (noon) at 5.40 p.m. the enemy exploded a mine under the 2) Worcesters front line. Enemy shelled our BOYAUS and Batt'n H.Q. with light H.V. guns at 20 minute intervals throughout the night.	
11	Quiet day with shelling, as before, at intervals through the night.	
12	Very wet and trenches kept sliding in very badly whole Batt'n working all day and throughout night. Enemy shelled Batt'n H.Q. at 3 a.m. night 12/13 and got a direct hit on the roof of the dug-out, without penetrating the roof. To casualties.	Lt Col H. St C. Wilkins took command of 5th Bde from this date during the absence of Br. Gen. Corkran on leave to England.
BEUVRY 13th	Relieved by 2/R. W. Fusiliers (19th Bde) by 12 noon The Batt'n went into billets at BEUVRY for the night.	
14	Paraded at 9.30 a.m. and marched to VENDIN where the	

J. A. Gape

Army Form C. 2118

WAR DIARY
or
INTELLIGENCE SUMMARY

(Erase heading not required.)

Instructions regarding War Diaries and Intelligence Summaries are contained in F. S. Regs., Part II. and the Staff Manual respectively. Title Pages will be prepared in manuscript.

Place	Date	Hour	Summary of Events and Information	Remarks and references to Appendices
VENDIN	15th		Batt: exchanged billets with the 2/ S. Staffordshire Regt. Ordinary Routine. 2 Lieut R. SLATTER posted to the Batt: on promotion from the 2nd Batt:	
	16th		Ordinary Routine.	
	17th		at 3 p.m. the Gas Expert (1st Army) lectured 200 N.C.O.s men of the Batt: and 200 of Glasgow Hghrs, a cylinder was then turned on in an out-house and all ranks filed through with Tube Helmets on.	
	18th		Ordinary Routine.	
	19th		" "	
	20th		" "	
	21st		" "	
	22nd		Batt: relieves the 2nd Batt: (27th D.) in Billets at HARLEY STREET.	
HARLEY ST. (3rd CAMBRN)	23rd to 25th		Relieved 2/ Oxfords in Section A1 from GUN STREET (inclusive) to RIDLEY WALK (exclusive) One Company of 21st R. Fusiliers attached on 28th for 24 hours duty	2Lt J.G.S MORRISON and T STRANGER joined 24th 2Lt R.P SLATTER joined 26th 2Lt S.E LUKIN joined 29th
Section A1	26th		Ordinary work. One Company of 21st R.F attached for 24 hours duty Casualty 1 wounded.	2Lt
	27th			
	28th			
	29th			

Army Form C. 2118

WAR DIARY
or
INTELLIGENCE SUMMARY
(Erase heading not required.)

Instructions regarding War Diaries and Intelligence Summaries are contained in F.S. Regs., Part II. and the Staff Manual respectively. Title Pages will be prepared in manuscript.

Place	Date	Hour	Summary of Events and Information	Remarks and references to Appendices
	30th		Batt'n relieved by 21 Oxfords and came into billets in BETHUNE. (RUE D'AIRE)	

5th Infantry Brigade.

2nd Division.

(Battn. transferred to
100 Bde. 33rd Div.
15.12.15)

WAR DIARY

1st BATTN. THE QUEEN'S (ROYAL WEST SURREY REGIMENT).

DECEMBER

1 9 1 5

WAR DIARY or INTELLIGENCE SUMMARY

Army Form C. 2118

Place	Date	Hour	Summary of Events and Information	Remarks and references to Appendices
BETHUNE	1st Dec		Draft of 61 Other Ranks joined.	
B1 Section	2nd		Batt: paraded at 9am and marched to PONT FIXE. Relief of 2/ H.L.I. completed by 1p.m. Right flank on canal, left flank near FINCHLEY ROAD. 1 Coy of 17th R. Fusiliers attached for 24 hours.	
"	3rd		Quiet day. 1 Coy of 17th R. Fusiliers attached for 24 hours.	
"	4th		Casualty. 1 wounded	
"	5th		--	
"	6th		Batt: relieved by 2/ Oxfords by 1.15p.m. and marched back to billets	
			─ BETHUNE. (Rue d'Aire)	
BETHUNE	7th	10.15am	Batt: paraded and marched to Ordnance Workers. Inspection of Gas drill.	
Section A1.	8th	9am	Batt: paraded and marched to CUINCHY where it relieved the Glasgow 14th in sector A1.- 6.30p.m. on night and 2/ H.L.I. on left. One company of 2/4th R.F. attached to the Batt: and holding the line in left front of A1. Casualties - 3 Lt. Col of 24th relieved by another Coy of same Regt. Art: Bombardment of enemy's front line was prepared though it was to have taken place from 10 a.m. to 3p.m. Ranes but all afternoon and night. Trenches very bad. Casualties 1 killed.	
	9th		Headquarters position - A1. occupied all morning. Only portions of front line were held and a limited number of Communication Trenches up & down, all work to be continued in future to maintain these potions. Batt: H.Q moved from WOBURN	
	10th		ABBEY to HARLEY STREET at 4p.m.	PM Copy

WAR DIARY or INTELLIGENCE SUMMARY

Army Form C. 2118

Place	Date	Hour	Summary of Events and Information	Remarks and references to Appendices
Sector A	Dec 11		Quiet day. Received orders for in relief tomorrow. Casualties 3 wounded.	
BEUVRY	12		One Coy of 1/13th Essex attached for 24 hours for Platoon Training. Relief by 2/8th Beds commenced at 10 a.m. and completed by 2 p.m. The Batt: marched back to Billets in BEUVRY. Casualties nil.	
BETHUNE	13		Batt: paraded at 10.30 A.M. and marched to Billets in the RUE D'AIRE at BETHUNE. Remainder of day occupied in cleaning up billets and preparing for G.O.C.'s inspection tomorrow.	
	14		The Batt: paraded at 10.0 a.m. in the square outside the SOUS PREFECTURE in BETHUNE. Major General WALKER addressed the Batt: and said goodbye on the occasion of then Transfer of to 33rd Div'n. The Batt: afterwards marched past.	
	15		Batt: paraded at 9.0 a.m. and marched to ST HILAIRE via CHOCQUES and LILLERS. Remainder of day occupied in settling into Billets. From this date the Batt: belongs to the 100 to 13th. (General Tn: J.O.)	
ST HILAIRE	16		Lt I.N.S SYMONS and one other rank joined the Batt: Brigade Route March at 10 a.m. The Batt: Class. Distance about 7½ miles.	
	17		Ordinary Routine.	
	18			
	19		Brigade Route March (about 4½ miles) commencing at 10.0 a.m. On J. FRENCH passed through the village at 11.10. The Batt: lined the streets at 11 a.m. Drum - Marching Order. (F.S.M.O.)	gas capt

Army Form C. 2118

WAR DIARY
or
INTELLIGENCE SUMMARY

(Erase heading not required.)

Instructions regarding War Diaries and Intelligence Summaries are contained in F. S. Regs., Part II. and the Staff Manual respectively. Title Pages will be prepared in manuscript.

Place	Date	Hour	Summary of Events and Information	Remarks and references to Appendices
ST HILAIRE.	20th		Ordinary routine	The J.T.Rumm and Lts George strength returns with S.O.D. & M.G. Cor d/21/12/15
—"—	21st		—"—	
—"—	22nd		Regtl Scheme for young officers all morning.	
—"—	23rd		Lieut-Colonel H. St.C. WILKINS proceeded to England for Staff duty. The Command of the Battn devolves on Major L.M. CROFTS.	
—"—	24th		Bombing accident during practice this morning owing to premature explosion of a 305 (MILLS) grenade. Casualties 1 Killed & 5 wounded. Draft of 1 Sergt and 45 other ranks joined the Battn at 2 p.m.	
—"—	25th		Ordinary Routine.	
—"—	26th		—"—	
—"—	27th		—"—	
BELLRUE	28th	AM 8.55	Paraded and marched via LILLERS and GONNEHEM to BELLRIVE. (9 miles.) Billeted here for the night.	
BETHUNE	29th	11.35	Paraded and marched via GONNEHEM and CHOCQUES to BETHUNE where the Battn billeted in MONT MORENCY Barracks.	JRR
—"—	30th		Ordinary Routine.	
—"—	31st		C.O. and Coy Commanders went to reconnoitre Sub-Sector A2 where the Battn will be occupying trenches on Jan 2nd 1916.	

L.M. Crofts Major
Comdg 1/ Queen's Regt